WHAT'S THE DEAL?

Alcohol

KT-558-277

NORWICH CITY COLLEGE
| | | |
|---|---|---|
| Stock No. | 247 194 | |
| Class | 613.81 BIN | |
| Cat. | Proc. | 3WL |

247 194

**Jane Bingham**

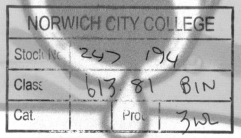

# www.heinemann.co.uk/library

Visit our website to find out more information about Heinemann Library books.

To order:

 Phone 44 (0) 1865 888066

Send a fax to 44 (0) 1865 314091

Visit the Heinemann Bookshop at www.heinemann.co.uk/library to browse our catalogue and order online.

Produced for Heinemann Library by
White-Thomson Publishing Ltd,
Bridgewater Business Centre,
210 High Street, Lewes,
East Sussex, BN7 2NH.

First published in Great Britain by Heinemann Library,
Jordan Hill, Oxford OX2 8EJ, part of Harcourt Education.

Heinemann Library is a registered trademark of
Harcourt Education Ltd.

© Harcourt Education Ltd 2006.
First published in paperback 2007.
The moral right of the proprietor has been asserted.

All rights reserved. No part of this publication may be
reproduced, stored in a retrieval system, or transmitted
in any form or by any means, electronic, mechanical,
photocopying, recording, or otherwise, without either
the prior written permission of the publishers or a
licence permitting restricted copying in the United
Kingdom issued by the Copyright Licensing Agency Ltd,
90 Tottenham Court Road, London W1T 4LP
(www.cla.co.uk).

Consultant: Jenny McWhirter, Head of Education and
   Prevention, DrugScope
Editorial: Clare Collinson
Design: Tim Mayer
Picture Research: Elaine Fuoco-Lang
Production: Duncan Gilbert

Originated by P.T. Repro Multi Warna
Printed and bound in China, by South China
   Printing Company.

The paper used to print this book comes from
sustainable resources.

The case studies and quotations in this book are
based on factual examples. However, in some cases,
the names or other personal information have been
changed to protect the privacy of the individual
concerned.

10 digit ISBN 0 431 10780 7 (hardback)
13 digit ISBN 978 0 431 10780 6 (hardback)
10 09 08 07 06
10 9 8 7 6 5 4 3 2 1

10 digit ISBN 0 431 10792 0 (paperback)
13 digit ISBN 978 0 431 10792 9 (paperback)
11 10 09 08 07
10 9 8 7 6 5 4 3 2 1

**British Library Cataloguing in Publication Data**
Bingham, Jane
   Alcohol. – (What's the deal?)
   1. Alcohol – Juvenile literature 2. Drinking of
   alcoholic beverages – Juvenile literature
   3. Alcoholism – Juvenile literature
   I. Title
   362.2'92
A full catalogue record for this book is available from
the British Library.

**Acknowledgements**
The publisher would like to thank the following for
their kind permission to use their photographs:

Alamy (Colin Edwards/Photofusion Picture Library)
**25**, (Nick Hanna) **12**, (PCL) **8–9**, (Pegaz) **11**; Corbis **16**,
**33**, (Paul Assaker) **13**, (Bernardo Bucci) **6**, (Robert
Essel NYC) **19**, (Randy Faris) **4–5**, (Gary Houlder) **26**,
(Tom and Dee Ann McCarthy) **45**, (Parrot
Pascal/Corbis Sygma) **42–43**, (Steve Prezant) **27**,
(RNT Productions) **17**, (Chuck Savage) **32**, **40**, (Sam
Sharpe) **22**, (Swim Ink) **20**, (Bill Varie) **29**; Harcourt
(Getty Images/PhotoDisc) **10**, **14**, **34**; Rex Features
(Nukari) **38–39**, (Sierankowski) **24**, **31**, (Sipa Press) **37**,
**41**; Science Photo Library (Gusto) **23**, (Cordelia
Molloy) **30**, (Jim Varney) **35**; Stockbyte **48**; Topfoto
(Danielle Austen/Syracuse Newspapers/The Image
Works) **46–47**, (Stuart Cohen/The Image Works) **18**,
(Bob Daemmrich/The Image Works) **7**, **51**, (FotoWare)
**15**, (Chet Gordon/The Image Works) **21**.

Cover artwork by Phil Weyman, Kralinator Design.

Every effort has been made to contact copyright
holders of any material reproduced in this book. Any
omissions will be rectified in subsequent printings if
notice is given to the publishers.

# Contents

❚ Words appearing in the text in bold, **like this**, are explained in the Glossary.

# Alcohol – what's the deal?

Rick was a promising student and an excellent athlete, and he had great plans for his life. But then he got involved with a group of friends who liked to drink alcohol. It started quite slowly, but soon Rick was drinking every day – and drinking heavily.

Before long, Rick's life started to change dramatically. He lost his job, crashed his car, and picked fights with all his friends. His girlfriend pleaded with him to give up drinking, but in the end she just gave up trying and left him.

The wake-up call came when Rick was admitted to hospital after collapsing with **inflammation** of the liver at the age of 24. His doctors struggled to save his life, and when he finally recovered they told him that unless he gave up drinking he would be dead within ten years. As he lay in his hospital bed, Rick took a long, hard look at his life. He had thrown away so many chances – and all because of alcohol. He told himself that if he wanted a future, he just had to stop drinking ... and he did it. Now Rick works at an alcohol recovery centre, where he helps other people to overcome their **addiction**. He tells all the young people he meets, "Things were pretty good for me before I started drinking ... and look what happened. Once you get hooked ... you're in trouble. Sometimes it's too late."

Rick's story is typical of lots of young people. What decisions will you make about alcohol?

### Surely it's OK?

Drinking alcohol is so much a part of our society that most people don't give it a second thought. People drink alcohol in restaurants and bars, at home, and at parties. Supermarket shelves are piled high with drink. Many of the images we see in the **media** send out the message that it's cool to drink.

### A serious problem

In fact, alcohol can be very dangerous. It affects your brain, changing the way you think and behave. It's easy to get "hooked" on alcohol and, when it's drunk in large quantities, it can have very serious health effects and even result in death. Drinking excessive amounts of alcohol can lead to violent behaviour. Driving under the influence of drink results in many innocent deaths every year. And **alcohol dependence** causes misery not just to **alcoholics**, but also to their families.

▌ Many people don't realize that they have a problem with alcohol until it's too late.

# A powerful drug

Alcohol is the world's most widely used drug. In fact, drinking alcohol is so widespread today that it's very easy to forget that it's a drug at all. But just because alcohol is everywhere, that doesn't mean that it's not dangerous. Based on a powerful chemical that affects the brain in minutes, alcohol changes the way people think and behave – and it can even lead to death through **alcohol poisoning**.

## What does alcohol do?

All alcoholic drinks contain a chemical called ethyl alcohol, or **ethanol** for short. When people drink alcohol, the ethanol passes through the wall of their stomach and into their bloodstream. It is carried to every cell of the body, including the brain, where it takes effect almost straightaway.

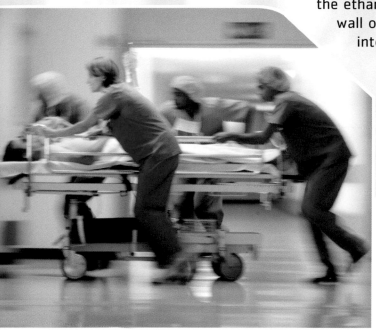

▌Alcohol poisoning often results in death, as the drinker stops breathing and enters a **coma**.

Even a very small amount of alcohol affects the brain's ability to concentrate. It also affects the body, making movements clumsier. And as the drinker takes more alcohol into his or her body, these mental and physical effects become much more extreme. If a drinker continues to drink more alcohol, the alcohol will gradually penetrate the brain until he or she develops alcohol poisoning. You can read a full description of the impact of alcohol on pages 24–25 of this book.

## What kind of drug is it?

Alcohol is a **depressant** drug, which means it slows down the body, making people clumsy and slurring their speech. It also slows down the mind, with the result that it's hard for drinkers to make quick judgements.

Some people question why alcohol is called a depressant, when one of its effects seems to be making drinkers feel more cheerful and outgoing. This happens because alcohol **suppresses** people's usual **inhibitions**, allowing them to behave in a way they wouldn't normally do. However, many drinkers find that these positive feelings don't last. As they continue to drink, their initial cheerfulness is replaced by feelings of depression.

### 🛈 Alcohol deaths

In the United States, 1 in every 20 deaths is caused by alcohol – making a total of more than 100,000 deaths each year.

▌ Drinking alcohol can change the way people behave – and it can ruin their chances of making a good impression!

# Different drinks

Put very simply, alcohol is made when food is allowed to ferment, or go mouldy. This fermentation process produces a liquid containing the chemical **ethanol** – or pure alcohol. Depending on the sort of method used, a range of different types of drink can be produced – and some drinks are much stronger than others!

## Different strengths

Each type of alcoholic drink contains a different amount of ethanol (pure alcohol). For example, beer and wine contain less ethanol than **spirits**, such as whisky, vodka, and gin.

But knowing the strength of a drink isn't always easy. Manufacturers sometimes produce a range of brands of different strengths. This is often the case with lagers. Today, many companies make extra-strong lagers that are labelled "special brew" or "export strength".

❚ There are a vast number of different drinks available and it's often quite hard to work out exactly how strong they are.

Spirits are very much stronger than other forms of alcohol. For example, gin and whisky contain about four times as much alcohol as wine. This means they have to be treated in a very different way. In bars and restaurants, spirits are always served in carefully measured small amounts (known as measures). Spirits are often mixed with a non-alcoholic drink, such as tonic water, to **dilute** the ethanol.

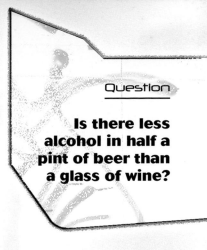

## Question

**Is there less alcohol in half a pint of beer than a glass of wine?**

## Measuring strengths

The strength of an alcoholic drink is often measured in terms of the amount of "Alcohol by Volume (AbV)". This is shown on the label as a percentage. For example, if a bottle or can is labelled "4% AbV", it means 4 per cent of the drink is pure ethanol. The higher the percentage, the stronger the drink will be. Beers usually contain about 3.5 to 5 per cent AbV, wine about 12 per cent and spirits about 40 per cent.

### ❗ Hidden danger

Recently, there has been a dramatic rise in the very dangerous practice of "**spiking**" alcoholic drinks with **sedative** drugs. Spiking is when people secretly add alcohol or other drugs to another person's drink. Sedative drugs, such as Rohypnol and Gamma Hydroxybutyrate (GHB), make the drinker very drowsy or even unconscious, putting them in danger of being sexually assaulted or raped. "Date rape", as it is often known, can happen to anyone – men as well as women. All drinkers need to watch out for people interfering with their drink. They should keep their drink with them at all times and never accept drinks from strangers.

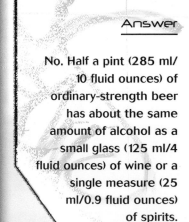

## Answer

No. Half a pint (285 ml/ 10 fluid ounces) of ordinary-strength beer has about the same amount of alcohol as a small glass (125 ml/4 fluid ounces) of wine or a single measure (25 ml/0.9 fluid ounces) of spirits.

# Alcohol in society

Like it or not, alcohol is everywhere in our society. In fact, it's so widespread that no one takes much notice of it – until it causes trouble. But **alcohol abuse** can cause major problems – costing huge sums of money and claiming innocent lives. Can you imagine how you would feel if someone in your family or one of your friends were injured or killed by a driver who'd had too much to drink?

## Different drinkers

For people in many countries, drinking alcohol is simply part of their everyday life. They may have a drink with friends after work, at dinner with their family, or before watching a football match. This kind of drinking in **moderation** doesn't do any serious harm and can make some people feel relaxed.

But there are other kinds of drinking that are very worrying. Some people go out at night determined to get drunk, and others may stay at home and drink until they're ill. Sometimes people simply don't notice how much they've been drinking until it's too late. In cases like these, alcohol becomes a serious problem – not just for the drinker, but also for society.

▌ People in many different cultures around the world celebrate special occasions by drinking alcohol. In traditional Jewish wedding ceremonies, it is customary for the bride and groom to sip from a glass or cup of wine.

## The downside of drink

Drinking excessive amounts of alcohol can lead to frightening and violent behaviour. After a heavy session of **binge drinking**, when people drink dangerously large amounts of alcohol, drinkers often get into arguments and fights. Sometimes they go on the rampage, trashing shops and offices and even private homes. Worst of all, driving under the influence of drink results in many thousands of deaths each year worldwide.

## A heavy cost

Many people are forced to pay for the alcohol-related problems in our society. Doctors and nurses have to work overtime caring for people with alcohol-related illnesses. The police are put at risk as they deal with dangerous situations fuelled by drink. Many people have their homes and businesses damaged as a result of alcohol-related violence. And businesses lose money when people are unable to work because of **hangovers** and other drink-related illnesses.

❚ When people drink alcohol in large quantities, things sometimes turn ugly.

## ⚠ Costs to society

A UK government report produced in 2004 found that:

- 17 million working days each year are lost because of hangovers and drink-related illness

- there are 1.2 million incidents of alcohol-related violence each year.

## Who drinks – and who doesn't?

People have been drinking alcohol for thousands of years – and the practice still continues today in many parts of the world. However, there are some people who make a deliberate decision not to drink any alcohol at all. Everyone should feel free to make their own decisions – and to do what's best for them.

## Drinking today

Nowadays, as in the past, people from a range of different cultures enjoy drinking in **moderation**. People drink to celebrate special occasions, to accompany their meals, to relax after work, and simply to be sociable with their friends and family. In some countries, it is traditional to celebrate weddings by drinking champagne. In many places – especially wine-producing nations like France, Spain, and Italy – people get together for large family meals that include the sharing of wine.

❚ In France, it's traditional
to drink wine at
family meals.

12

▌These two friends are enjoying a glass of tea together – a common custom in Muslim countries.

## Saying no

Although drinking is widespread in our society, not everyone chooses to drink. Some people simply don't like the taste, or find that drinking alcohol makes them feel unwell. Others decide they don't like the feeling of not being entirely in control of their bodies. For some people, drinking alcohol simply doesn't fit in with their religious beliefs. Strict Muslims do not drink any alcohol, and Sikhs and Buddhists also avoid it.

## Other reasons for avoiding drink

Some people make the decision not to drink because of something that has happened in their lives. They may have had a bad experience with alcohol, or a member of their family may have problems with drink. Sometimes, people make the decision not to drink after they have witnessed an accident caused by alcohol.

# Viewpoints

Dominic is thirteen and lives in France. His family usually drink a little wine with their meals, and for Dominic this is just part of normal family life. Ken, a paramedic working in a tough inner-city area, has had a completely different experience of alcohol. He has seen many lives wrecked by people who drink and drive, and for this reason has decided not to drink at all.

- **Drinking alcohol in moderation does no harm**
"In my family, we often drink a little wine with our dinner. Nobody drinks too much. It's just part of the experience of having an enjoyable time."
*Dominic*

- **Alcohol is dangerous – it's best to avoid it**
"I used to drink, but since I joined the ambulance team, I've given up. I've seen so many accidents caused by alcohol that I don't feel like drinking any more."
*Ken*

**What do you think?**

# Alcohol and the law

Most countries have laws about where alcohol can be sold, and where and when people are allowed to drink. The police enforce strict penalties to prevent **drink-driving**. Governments also try to control the age at which young people can start drinking. Of course it's important to have laws to control drinking and the sale of alcohol – but not everyone agrees about all of these laws.

## Selling alcohol

In most countries, only certain shops are allowed to sell alcohol to their customers. These shops are issued with a licence that gives them the right to sell alcohol to be consumed off the premises. In return for this licence, shopkeepers have a legal duty not to sell alcohol to anyone who is under a certain age.

## Serving alcohol

There are also laws about serving alcoholic drinks. Bars and pubs are granted a licence that gives them the right to serve alcohol on their premises. Restaurants also need a licence to serve drink with food. It is an offence for bar staff and restaurant owners to serve alcohol to a customer who is **under age** or who has had too much to drink. In most places, bars also have to keep to strict **opening hours**.

▌ Restaurants have to obey strict laws about serving alcohol to their customers. If they break these laws, their licence to serve alcohol can be taken away.

■ Sometimes, drivers who are suspected of drink-driving may be asked to take a "sobriety test", which involves trying to walk in a straight line.

## Drink-driving laws

Most countries have very strict laws against drinking and driving. In the United Kingdom, Australia, and the United States, drivers suspected of dangerous driving can be stopped and tested on the spot. Drivers may have to blow into a **breathalyser**, which registers the amount of alcohol in their body. If they are over the limit, they are usually disqualified from driving for a period. They may also be given heavy fines or sent to prison (see also pages 46–47).

### ⚠ Alcohol arrests

According to a recent UK survey, around half of all violent crimes are committed by people under the influence of alcohol.

## Viewpoints

In many countries, the laws on opening hours are becoming more relaxed, and pubs and bars are opening for longer. But not everyone agrees that this is the right thing to do.

● **Bars should have short opening hours**

If opening hours were shorter people would drink less and people in bars would have less time to get drunk.

● **Opening hours should be longer**

It might be safer for bars to stay open longer. When opening hours are restricted, people sometimes drink dangerous amounts in a short period of time.

**What do you think?**

# Under-age drinking

**Under-age** drinking is a growing concern in our society, but it's not an easy problem to solve. Everyone agrees that it can be very harmful for young people to drink alcohol too soon, but what is it that makes it so dangerous and at what age is it safe to start?

▌ It can be very tempting to go out drinking with friends. But heavy drinking can easily lead to lower grades at school and more limited choices for the future.

## A major problem

Under-age drinking is a worrying problem for several reasons. When young people drink heavily before their bodies are fully developed they can cause permanent damage to their livers (see page 26). They are also putting themselves at risk in other ways. Once under the influence of alcohol, they are less able to make sensible decisions. As a result, they are more likely to become the victims of crime, take physical risks, and become involved in fights.

*"I still have nightmares about what I did to my friends. I'm sure that crash will stay with me for the rest of my life."*

Lee, a college student, who was involved in a **drink-driving** accident, killing one of his friends and injuring another

## Danger on the road

Every day of the year, inexperienced teenage drivers take to the road while they are under the influence of alcohol. They take terrible chances with their own lives and those of their friends – and also run the risk of killing and injuring total strangers. Just imagine how it would feel to be the young driver – always living with the memory of what you'd done.

## Deciding limits

In different parts of the world, governments have come to different decisions about the minimum drinking age. In the United Kingdom and Australia, the legal age for buying alcohol is 18. In Japan, the minimum age is 20, while in the United States the legal age limit in all states is 21. In some European countries, the age limit is lower than elsewhere. Young people in France, for example, are allowed to buy alcoholic drinks from the age of 16.

## What's the right age?

Some people argue that a minimum legal drinking age of 21 is too high. They say that if 18-year-olds are considered old enough to vote in elections, get married, or fight in a war, then they are also old enough to drink alcohol. However, others claim that a higher age limit saves lives. They say that young people go through a lot of changes between the ages of 18 and 21, and by the time they reach 21, they are in a much better position to make sensible decisions about alcohol. (For more on the effects of alcohol on young people, see pages 26–27.)

▌Young people make lots of choices for themselves. Most young people under the legal drinking age make the decision to enjoy themselves without drinking alcohol.

# Why do people drink?

Why do so many people choose to drink, and why do they keep on drinking once they've started? It's worth taking a careful look at the reasons why people choose to drink alcohol.

## Why start?

For some young people, the first taste of alcohol happens at home on a special family occasion. However, many people have their first experience of drinking with their friends. Their mates may encourage them to try a drink, or they may just want to be like the rest of the gang. They may also think that drinking seems cool. Many advertisements send out the message that if you drink a particular product, it will somehow make you a more exciting person. But do you really think that this is true?

## Something to do?

A lot of people drink because they are bored, and for some people, drinking becomes a habit. Some environments, such as bars or clubs, encourage people to drink alcohol without really thinking about it. But individuals can always make the decision not to drink alcohol.

❚ Meeting up with friends doesn't have to involve drinking alcohol.

■ When people are feeling low, alcohol can sometimes seem to be the answer. But heavy drinking only makes things worse.

Drinking can easily become automatic – just something to do at a certain time of day or in a certain place. And once it has become a habit, it's hard to stop. It can also prevent you from finding more interesting things to do.

## The great escape?

Drinkers often say they drink to "escape". Some people turn to alcohol to help them get away from their problems, or to make them feel better about themselves. But this is not a solution. Even if the problems seem to disappear for a while, alcohol doesn't make them go away. Spending lots of time and money on drinking is actually the worst way to deal with problems.

### Kate's story

Kate had a job she loved, but then she was made **redundant**. At first she thought that drinking would make her feel better, but soon she was drinking all day long. By the time Kate realized how bad her problem was, she had lost all her confidence and most of her friends. Eventually, she joined a **rehabilitation** programme. She managed to stop drinking and gradually returned to normal, healthy life.

# Alcohol in the spotlight

Alcohol appears in the **media** all the time – and it's often presented in a very positive light. Advertisements send out the message that drinking is fun, and glamorous celebrities are often shown enjoying a drink. However, the media also shows the downside of alcohol, and many famous figures have revealed their drinking problems.

▌ Advertisers are very clever at making their products seem glamorous and sexy.

## The advertisers' message

Even though alcohol is a drug that can be very dangerous, advertisements for alcohol are everywhere – on TV, in magazines, and on billboards. The main message of all these advertisements is that drinking alcohol is fun. Commercials for alcohol usually show attractive people drinking in exotic places, or lively characters having a good time. Many of these images are specially designed to appeal to young people.

## Famous faces

One of the ways in which alcohol manufacturers encourage people to buy their products is by identifying their brands with famous figures. Companies pay huge sums to show a celebrity drinking their brand of alcohol, in the hope that the public will want to try it too. This method of persuasion is often used in commercials. It is also used, very cleverly, in films and TV programmes, when a favourite character is shown with a certain brand of drink. This subtle form of advertising is known as "product placement".

> "I numbed myself and poisoned myself for so many years, only to find out that it's really selfish and dumb."
>
> Actor Johnny Depp, who gave up a heavy drinking habit

▌ Although sports stars are often used to promote alcohol, many top athletes don't drink at all. They have a carefully controlled diet and think that drinking alcohol may harm their performance.

## A different story

However, not all images of alcohol in the media are positive ones. Sometimes a film glamorizing alcohol is followed by a news report clearly revealing the downside of drink. More documentaries are being made about the problems related to alcohol and **drink-driving**, and some feature films also show the dark side of alcohol.

The real-life stories of celebrities often reveal the negative aspects of drinking, as countless famous figures confess to their **addictions**. In recent years, stars like Jack Osbourne, Matthew Perry, and Drew Barrymore have spoken publicly about their problems with drink. Many famous names from the world of music, sport, and cinema have been forced to spend time out of their careers, trying to give up alcohol and get their lives back on track.

# The alcohol business

Alcohol is very big business. It brings in vast sums of money, both for the manufacturers who produce it and for the retailers who sell it. Pubs and bars also profit from high sales of alcohol, and all these groups work hard to push their product to the public.

❚ This car may be advertising a famous beer, but the driver at the wheel would never dream of combining alcohol with driving.

## The sports connection

Alcohol companies pour a huge amount of money into sports – contributing to the costs of building new stadiums and sponsoring competitions. In return they get a massive amount of free publicity, as stadiums and players' shirts are plastered with their company name. Sports **sponsorship** also makes people connect a particular sport with a certain brand of drink. However, sports stars aiming for peak performance probably never touch the stuff!

## Pushing the product

Alcohol companies work very hard to make sure their product reaches the largest possible number of people. One way to achieve this is to encourage certain groups of people to buy more alcohol. In particular, some manufacturers have concentrated on women and younger people – groups that have traditionally spent less on alcohol.

## Targeting youth

Over recent years, alcohol manufacturers have produced a new kind of drink – **alcopops**. These appeal especially to young people. A mix of fruit juice and **spirits**, they taste very sweet and may appear as harmless as soft drinks. In fact, alcopops are stronger than many beers. Although the manufacturers deny that alcopops are designed specifically to appeal to young people, their "funky" packaging and names send out a very different message.

## Special offers and happy hours

It's not just manufacturers who try to push their products. Some retailers have special offers, such as "buy one get one free". These offers can encourage people to buy more alcohol than they had intended to. They may even make people buy some alcohol when they hadn't planned to buy any at all. Similarly, many pubs and bars have "**happy hours**" when they sell cut-price drinks.

## Viewpoints

Many people think that happy hours should be banned, but others disagree.

- **Happy hours are dangerous**

Happy hours can make people drink more than they planned in a shorter space of time. They usually take place in the early evening, and this can encourage customers to start on a long night of drinking.

- **Bars should be free to have happy hours**

Like any other business, bars have to survive and win customers. This means they should be able to run promotions, just like other businesses. It's up to the customers to act responsibly and make their own decisions.

**What do you think?**

▌With their bright, enticing colours, alcopops like these are deliberately marketed to appeal to younger drinkers.

# What does alcohol do?

Alcohol begins to affect the body within five to ten minutes of the first sip, as the chemical **ethanol** enters the bloodstream and travels to the brain. The effects become increasingly intense as the drinker takes in more alcohol. If a drinker continues to take in large quantities, they may suffer **alcohol poisoning** and even die.

## Early effects

Even just one drink (a small glass of wine or half a pint of beer) can affect the brain's ability to concentrate, slowing down reaction times and making it harder to make accurate judgements. It also makes people lose their **inhibitions**, so they may say and do things that they wouldn't normally do.

▌ After several drinks, people lose control of their movements and start to feel dizzy and sick.

## Do the effects of alcohol get stronger?

As a person drinks more alcohol, the level of ethanol in their bloodstream rises, and its effects on their brain increase. People lose the ability to coordinate or control their movements, slurring their words and becoming clumsy. After a few drinks, ethanol seriously affects a person's ability to perform physical tasks, such as driving.

If someone continues to drink more alcohol, the effects become even stronger. People start to talk very loudly and they may get into arguments or become tearful or angry. Their vision is also affected – they may

## Question

**What should you do if someone becomes unconscious after drinking heavily?**

have difficulty focusing and see two of everything. They may feel giddy or find it hard to stand up and walk. They may vomit and also lose control of their bladder. Some people lose consciousness, passing out completely as they enter the early stages of alcohol poisoning.

## Alcohol poisoning

Alcohol poisoning happens when the level of alcohol in the brain becomes so high that it stops the brain cells from functioning. At this stage, the drinker's life is in serious danger, and they may enter a state of deep unconsciousness called a **coma**. In some cases, the brain stops sending signals to the body to breathe, and the drinker may die.

Alcohol poisoning can happen to anyone who drinks a very large amount of alcohol, but people are particularly at risk if they drink large quantities in a short space of time. And alcohol poisoning doesn't just affect people who drink regularly. It can even happen the first time someone drinks alcohol.

▌ If a drinker reaches the stage of passing out, they are in serious danger and need experienced medical help immediately.

Answer

Call the emergency services straightaway — the person's life is in danger and they need medical attention.

## Different drinkers

Although the effects of alcohol are much the same on everyone, some people are more strongly affected than others. A drinker's size and sex are both important factors in the way that alcohol works on their body, and young people are at special risk.

## Size matters

Alcohol takes effect by spreading into the bloodstream, where it is **diluted** with other body fluids, which are mainly made up of water. The smaller a person's body is, the less water it contains and the more **concentrated** the alcohol is inside it. This means that a small person needs less alcohol than a large person in order to feel its physical effects. It is one of the reasons why drinking alcohol is especially dangerous for young people, who are usually smaller and lighter than adults.

## Age matters

Apart from the question of body size, young people are especially vulnerable to alcohol because their bodies are not completely developed. **Under-age** drinking puts a serious strain on the liver, which is forced to deal with an overload of **toxins** (poisons) before it has reached its full adult size. Young, developing brains are also put in great danger.

▌Young women who drink heavily risk doing permanent damage to their liver and brain.

## Brain damage

Scientists have discovered that the brain doesn't stop growing until a person is around twenty. The area responsible for making complex judgements is one of the last to mature. This means that young people who drink often and heavily are likely to cause permanent damage to this vital part of their brain. How do you think it would feel to know that you had damaged your brain forever before you were twenty years old?

▌ Alcohol affects some people more strongly than others, and young people and women are especially at risk.

## Sex matters

Women are usually affected by alcohol more quickly than men, because their bodies are smaller and contain less water. When health experts advise on safe levels of drinking, they always suggest lower levels for women than men.

Young women drinkers are in a very high-risk group because they combine two factors – their smaller body size and the fact that their liver and brain have not yet fully matured. When you add to these risk factors the fact that young women often choose to drink strong drinks (such as **spirits** or **alcopops**), it becomes clear that they are putting themselves in serious danger.

## Other factors

As well as size, age, and sex, there are other factors that affect the way the body responds to alcohol. The amount that someone has eaten before they start drinking, how quickly they drink, and whether they are used to drinking or not all make a difference to the way alcohol affects them. People with very little experience of drinking are especially at risk, while drinking on an empty stomach makes people get drunk faster – and feel worse afterwards.

## The morning after

Alcohol doesn't just have an immediate impact. It also takes a long time to work its way through the body, and the later effects of drinking are very unpleasant. All heavy drinkers know the agony of a **hangover**, as their body recovers from the effects of alcohol and really starts to hurt.

Question

**How long does it take for the body to rid itself of alcohol after a heavy drinking session?**

*"I'll never forget how I felt the next morning. I just lay in bed and wanted to die. It even hurt to move my head off the pillow."*

Naomi, a college student, remembering a bad hangover

Answer

48 hours.

### Feeling ill

Alcohol is a **diuretic**, which means that it takes water from the body, causing people to urinate frequently. This results in **dehydration** – a severe headache, a very dry mouth, and even a swollen tongue. People suffering from hangovers usually feel sick and have an upset stomach. They also often find that bright light hurts their eyes and loud noises hurt their head.

### Feeling regret

People often say and do things when they are drinking that they later regret. In particular, many people make bad decisions about sex while they are under the influence of drink. They may go to bed with someone and have unprotected sex, which could result in an unwanted pregnancy or in contracting a sexually transmitted infection (**STI**).

### Memory blackouts

It's quite common for people to have no memory at all of whole stretches of time that passed while they were under the influence of drink. These memory "blackouts" mean they have no idea where they've been or what they've said and done. Can you imagine how scary it must be to wake up with absolutely no idea of what happened the night before?

▌ Hangovers don't just make you feel terrible. They also make you miss out on a lot of fun while you're waiting to feel human again.

## Lost days

It takes at least a day to recover from a bad hangover – which means the whole day has been wasted. Heavy drinkers often need to take days off work. If someone is always recovering from the night before, they can miss out on some good times.

# Longer-term effects

After people have been drinking heavily for a while, the alcohol begins to have some noticeable long-term effects on their bodies. It also affects their moods and their ability to concentrate.

Alcohol is full of **calories**, so when people start to drink large amounts they often put on weight. Beer drinkers in particular may develop a characteristic "beer belly". However, some drinkers lose weight instead. They may be missing out on proper meals because of their drinking, or because of **hangovers**. Heavy drinking can also cause stomach **ulcers** – open sores which make eating difficult and painful.

I Would you like to have a body like this? Regular drinking sessions soon start to have an effect on people's bodies.

## Liver, heart, and brain

Heavy drinking damages all the organs of the body, but especially the liver – the organ that breaks down alcohol and gets rid of its **toxins** from the body. The average liver can only cope with 7.9 grams (0.3 ounces) of pure alcohol an hour – the amount of alcohol in about half a pint of beer or a small glass of wine. When people drink a large amount of alcohol each day, their liver never gets a break and becomes damaged.

### ! Breast cancer risk

Recent studies have shown that there is an increased risk of breast cancer among heavy women drinkers.

I Heavy drinking can lead to depression and other mental health problems.

Alcohol also makes the heart beat faster, which speeds up the rate at which the blood travels round the body. In the long term, this can cause problems with **circulation**, and can also result in dangerously high **blood pressure**. It is also responsible for the flushed complexion and broken veins that are characteristic of many heavy drinkers.

Drinking large quantities of alcohol affects the brain, causing a range of symptoms such as sleeplessness, depression, **panic attacks**, and memory loss. You can read more about the long-term health problems caused by alcohol on pages 36–37.

### Fertility

Alcohol also affects drinkers' **fertility**. Large doses of alcohol make it difficult for men to get an erection, and men who drink heavily also have a dramatically reduced **sperm** count. Women also experience decreased fertility if they drink heavily, and drinking during pregnancy can damage the unborn child (see pages 42–43).

### Gary's story

Gary was a talented footballer with a steady girlfriend and a great bunch of mates. He liked going out in the evenings to have a few beers, but soon he was drinking much more than his friends. He began to pile on weight and was dropped from the football team. When his girlfriend left him, he realized that he had to do something fast, and he made the decision to stop drinking altogether.

# Binge drinking

Sometimes, people drink far too much. They keep on drinking alcohol until they are completely out of control. This kind of excessive drinking is usually known as "**binge drinking**".

## ⚠ Emergency action

If you suspect that someone has drunk a dangerous amount of alcohol, there are several things you can do.

- Call for help. There'll probably be people around who've had more experience than you.

- If the drinker's breathing is irregular, if they appear to be unconscious, or if their skin has a bluish tinge, call the emergency services straightaway. If the drinker has vomited, or seems sleepy and listless, roll them on to their side to prevent them from choking.

- Even if the drinker appears to have recovered, don't leave them alone. Sometimes serious medical problems develop later.

And remember – if you're in any doubt, always call for help.

## What is binge drinking?

Binge drinking involves consuming dangerously large amounts of alcohol in a single session, usually with the deliberate aim of getting drunk.

Binge drinking usually takes place in groups, but sometimes people drink alone.

❚ People often drink to keep up with their mates, but people should always feel free to make their own decisions.

Do you think this looks like a fun night out? All too often, binge drinking sessions end up with people being really ill.

This can be extremely dangerous if the drinker passes out and there is no one around to help. Traditionally, groups of young men have indulged in binge drinking, and this practice continues today. But nowadays some young women also drink massive amounts. Unlike male drinkers, who often stick to beer, women frequently choose to drink **spirits** – with the result that they often become even more unwell than the men.

## Why do people binge?

Sometimes young people drink excessively just to keep up with the group. Their mates may keep on urging them to have another drink. In this situation, members of a group sometimes keep on drinking long after they would really like to stop. However, everyone needs to make their own decision about drinking, and "real" friends will let you do what's right for you.

Some people over-indulge in alcohol to escape from reality. By becoming so drunk that they no longer remember anything, drinkers blot out their worries for a while. But the next day all the worries return, with the added problems caused by the night before.

## Bad consequences

The consequences of binge drinking can be extremely serious. Drinkers may become extremely ill, and even die from **alcohol poisoning** (see page 25). They may also be involved in dangerous accidents, or go to bed with someone and have unprotected sex, putting themselves at risk of an unwanted pregnancy or of catching **STIs**. And it's not just the drinkers who suffer from binge drinking. Sometimes property is damaged or innocent people are hurt.

# Alcohol dependence

For some people, the need for alcohol becomes the most important thing in their life. It takes over everything, making them forget their interests and their friends. It also wrecks their health, and often leads to early death. **Alcohol dependence** is a very serious problem, both for the individuals who suffer from it and for all the people around them.

I People who are alcohol-dependent need regular doses just to help them get through the day.

## Question

**Which kind of people are most likely to become alcohol-dependent?**

## What is alcohol dependence?

Many people manage to control their drinking. They are able to drink in **moderation** and can stop whenever they want. But others simply can't give up, and gradually their bodies come to require larger and larger amounts of alcohol. These people don't drink alcohol for pleasure, but because their bodies can't manage without it. People with this condition are often known as **alcoholics**, but they may also be described as "alcohol-dependent" because their bodies have come to depend on regular doses of alcohol.

## Psychological dependence

Alcohol dependence involves the mind as well as the body. Heavy drinkers become dependent on alcohol for its **psychological** effects. When they are deprived of alcohol, they may become very anxious, depressed, and withdrawn, and may also suffer from **panic attacks**.

## Why do people become alcohol-dependent?

There are many reasons why people become dependent on drink. Some people turn to alcohol because of something very stressful that has happened in their lives, such as a death in the family or a family break-up.

## ⚠ Psychological dependence

When someone is psychologically dependent on a drug, they rely on the drug because of the way it affects their emotions and their moods.

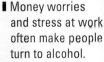
▌Money worries and stress at work often make people turn to alcohol.

Others may drink to get away from problems at work, and some start drinking heavily because they feel lonely.

Sometimes the reasons for becoming drink-dependent aren't so clear cut. Someone may start drinking a lot with their friends, and then only gradually realize that they have a problem.

### A family problem?

Health studies have proved that alcohol dependence often runs in families. It has been estimated that the children of alcoholics are up to seven times more likely than other people to become alcohol-dependent themselves. This may be partly due to an inherited tendency. However, the children of alcoholics may also turn to alcohol because they have been brought up in a home where people drink a lot.

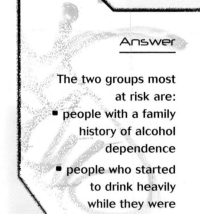

### Answer

The two groups most at risk are:
- people with a family history of alcohol dependence
- people who started to drink heavily while they were very young.

35

Drinking large amounts of alcohol over a period of years has a dramatic impact on the drinker's body, causing a range of life-threatening problems. **Alcohol abuse** also affects the mind, leading to depression and anxiety. All these effects make people who are **alcohol-dependent** extremely unwell.

## Damaging the body ...

Long-term alcohol abuse can make the drinker put on weight or become much thinner (see page 30). It causes problems with **circulation**, and can lead to bleeding **ulcers** in the stomach, and cancer of the mouth and throat. Heavy drinking also results in an increase in heart size, weakening of the heart muscle, abnormal heart rhythms, a risk of blood clots forming inside the heart, and a greatly increased risk of suffering a stroke. Heavy drinking in women has been linked to an increased risk of breast cancer. But the most dramatic effect of all is on the liver. Over a period of years, the once-healthy tissue in a drinker's liver is permanently damaged and gradually destroyed in a process called **cirrhosis**. Eventually, the liver ceases to function, and the drinker collapses and often dies.

## ... And the mind

Drinking large quantities of alcohol damages the brain, causing permanent memory loss and affecting the ability to concentrate. Many drinkers also suffer from crippling depression and anxiety. In extreme cases, alcohol-dependents may experience **hallucinations**, as the brain becomes poisoned by alcohol.

## Withdrawal symptoms

Once someone is used to drinking large amounts of alcohol, it can be very difficult and even dangerous to stop drinking. **Withdrawal** from alcohol can lead to a range of symptoms including profound anxiety, stomach cramps, sleeplessness, tremors (sometimes known as "the shakes"), and hallucinations. In extreme cases, a drinker may even suffer life-threatening fits. For all these reasons, withdrawal from alcohol abuse needs to be supervised by a doctor or some other medically qualified person.

## Chris's story

Chris started drinking heavily in her mid twenties, after a long-term relationship came to an end. She dropped out of her job and gradually lost touch with her family and friends. Her neighbour raised the alarm when he realized he hadn't seen her for over a week. Chris was discovered unconscious on her living-room floor and was rushed into hospital immediately. She was suffering from acute liver failure, **dehydration**, and malnutrition. For the previous few weeks, she'd lived almost entirely on alcohol, literally drinking herself to death. It was the fifth time she'd been taken into hospital, but this time it was too late. Chris died a few hours later, aged only 32.

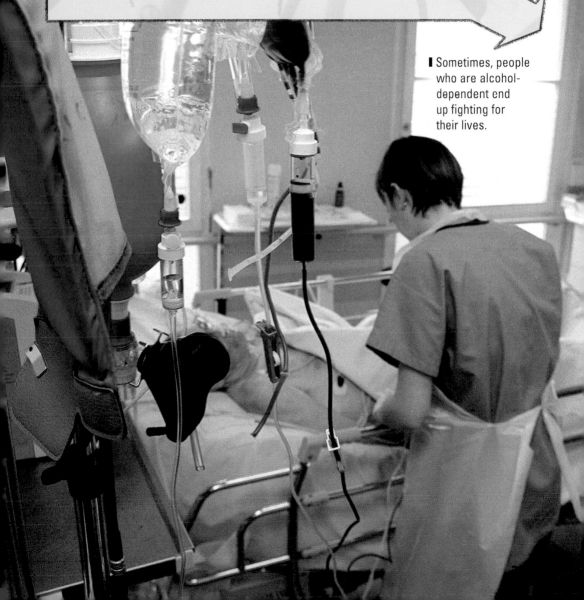

▮ Sometimes, people who are alcohol-dependent end up fighting for their lives.

# A drinker's day

After someone has become **alcohol-dependent**, their days start to take on a similar pattern. The first half of the day is spent recovering from the previous night. Then the drinking starts again, until the day ends with the drinker "crashing out". Meanwhile, work and other interests take second place to drinking. Living your life with drink as a constant companion is just no joke.

## The morning after

For most heavy drinkers, the day begins with a **hangover**. They have a splitting headache and an upset stomach, and there is a strong temptation to stay in bed and sleep off the effects of the night before, instead of getting up and going off to work. Some very heavy drinkers deal with this feeling by having another drink, and starting the day's drinking really early.

## Daytime drinking

If the heavy drinker manages to make it in to work, they drag themselves through the morning, nursing a hangover. Concentration is not easy and very little work gets done. Then, when lunchtime comes, they start to drink again. Working in the afternoon is not productive and they probably feel very tired from the night before.

## Crashing out

Evenings for an alcohol-dependent often feature a visit to a bar, but they may simply involve staying at home to drink. Either way, the drinker probably doesn't bother to have anything sensible to eat.

*"Sometimes when I look back on the week, all the days blur into one. I just don't know what I'm doing with my life."*

Mark, a heavy drinker, who has been alcohol-dependent for several years

During the course of the evening's drinking, the alcohol-dependent person will become less and less in touch with the people around them, and by the end of the evening they may need help getting to bed. They will then spend a restless night before the whole cycle begins again.

## Alcohol and work

It is very common for people with alcohol problems to lose their jobs. Employers who suspect their employees are drinking heavily are likely to give them notice to leave. Once a drinker no longer has to go out to work, the temptations to drink in the day are very strong. This is also the situation that faces many drinkers who are stuck at home for many hours.

❚ Instead of going shopping for groceries, some heavy drinkers simply stock up on alcohol.

# Getting help

The most important step towards recovery from **alcohol dependence** is for the drinker to admit they have a problem. Once they have recognized that they need help, there are a range of people and organizations that can help them with the process of recovery.

## Treatment and help

People with drinking problems may be treated in hospital or in a special community-based unit that specializes in problems related to alcohol. There are also specialist clinics, or **rehabilitation** centres. These clinics and centres help recovering **alcoholics** withdraw from alcohol, offer them support, and give them advice and encouragement on how to manage their alcohol problem in the future.

## Drying out

The first stage of treatment for a recovering alcoholic is the process of giving up alcohol, sometimes known as "drying out". **Withdrawal** from alcohol can be very difficult and drinkers often need medication to help them deal with its painful symptoms. They may also need medical treatment for conditions such as liver and stomach problems, caused by years of heavy drinking.

❚ For many people who are alcohol-dependent, picking up the phone to ask for help is the first step in changing their life.

## Psychological help

As well as medical assistance, people need **psychological** support, to help see them through the experience of drying out. Talking through their problems and difficulties with a trained counsellor helps to give people who are recovering from alcohol dependence the strength they need to keep on with the process of recovery.

## Giving up alcohol

For most people who have become drink-dependent, the only way they can deal with their problem is to give up drink altogether. Just a single drink can be enough to start them back on the road to dependence, so giving up completely is the only way that they can be sure their problem will not return.

Giving up alcohol can be very hard, especially in times of stress, and this is where discussion and counselling play a valuable part. As well as professional psychologists and counsellors, there are many voluntary organizations that offer help and support. Organizations such as Alcoholics Anonymous (AA for short) provide recovering alcoholics with a network of support, including telephone helplines and discussion groups.

*"What I have to do is live, not one day at a time, not one hour at a time, but one minute at a time. I have to work my program. If I don't, I won't last. I'll be dragged down ... That's what it means to be an alcoholic ... Recovery is an ongoing, lifelong process. Still, mine is a happy ending."*

Drew Barrymore, describing her fight against alcohol dependence in her autobiography, *Little Girl Lost*

▌Screen star Drew Barrymore battled with alcohol **addiction** throughout her teens. Now she has overcome her drinking problems.

# Alcohol and others

The problems caused by alcohol don't just end with the drinker. **Alcohol abuse** has a dramatic impact on the drinker's family and friends, and sometimes the effects reach even further than that. Alcohol can have a devastating effect on many innocent lives, even those of unborn babies.

## Alcohol and pregnancy

Alcohol in a pregnant woman's bloodstream circulates around the **foetus** (the growing baby) and interferes with its supply of oxygen and nourishment from the mother's body. Even small amounts of alcohol drunk by pregnant women can result in babies with low birth weight. Women who drink heavily risk having babies with a serious condition called "foetal alcohol syndrome". Many of these babies face a lifetime of operations and medical care.

## Turning nasty

There's no question about it – drinking large amounts of alcohol can lead to violence. Alcohol **suppresses** drinkers' **inhibitions** and also affects their judgement. This dangerous combination can result in aggressive behaviour, as drinkers pick fights and then refuse to "back off".

Sometimes groups of drinkers take to the streets, apparently determined to cause trouble. They may threaten innocent passers-by or vandalize property. In some cities and towns, alcohol-fuelled violence is a growing problem, and ordinary citizens may feel afraid to venture out late at night.

Sadly, sporting events may sometimes be the focus for alcohol-fuelled violence, as fans drink heavily before and during a match and then set out to let off their pent-up feelings. In the United Kingdom, soccer hooliganism is a serious problem. The police have taken drastic action, banning fans known to drink heavily from matches. In the United States, the authorities at major baseball games have been forced to take action because of the behaviour of drunken fans. Many of the 26 Major League baseball stadiums have "family" sections in which no alcohol is sold, while most stadiums prohibit the sale of alcohol after a certain time in the game.

❙ When people drink heavily, sporting rivalry can turn violent. Here, two groups of soccer supporters clash on the street.

# Alcohol and the family

When someone has a problem with drink, their whole family suffers. Everyone in the family worries about the drinker's health and has to live with their moods. There are also financial worries and fears about **drink-driving** and violence. The whole family lives in a permanent state of anxiety, not knowing what the drinker will do next.

## Question

**Is there anyone young people can contact to talk about drink problems in their family?**

## Answer

Yes. Look on pages 50–51 for advice about people to contact and pages 54–55 for a list of organizations and telephone helplines.

## A different person

People who live with someone who is **alcohol-dependent** often notice a change in their personality, as the need to drink becomes the most important thing in their life. Heavy drinkers often become bad-tempered or withdrawn.

People who are dependent on alcohol may also be extremely secretive, lying to their family in order to disguise the seriousness of their habit. Sometimes, drinkers are so desperate for a drink that they will even steal money from members of their family.

## Violence and money

Families of people with a serious drink problem can sometimes be on the receiving end of violence. It can be very frightening for partners and children when a drinker returns home ready to have a go at anyone who disagrees with them.

Alcohol dependence brings financial worries too. Alcohol is expensive, so the cost of buying drinks puts a strain on the family budget. Heavy drinkers often lose their jobs, and even if this hasn't happened, there is always the danger that it might.

## Taking on the burden

In many families where a parent drinks, the children are forced to take on lots of responsibility. Older children may feel that it is up to them to care for their younger brothers and sisters, to cook for the family, and to keep the house clean and tidy.

The children may also have the role of comforting their parent, and may even have to look after them when alcohol makes them ill. This is a heavy burden for a young person to bear, at an age when most of their friends are free to enjoy themselves. It can also be very scary. If you have to take care of someone in your family like this, it's always best to ask for help.

▌ It can be very frightening when someone you love turns violent.

# Drinking and driving

One of the most tragic effects of alcohol on our society is the number of deaths caused by **drink-driving**. Every year, many thousands of innocent people around the world are injured or killed in accidents involving drivers who are under the influence of alcohol. Is there anything that can be done to stop this dreadful waste of lives?

## Danger on the roads

It is an undisputed medical fact that drinking alcohol affects the brain. It slows down reaction times, so makes it harder to perform hand, arm, and leg movements. Drinking also affects mood and judgement, and people under the influence of alcohol often take risks that they would not consider if they were **sober**.

Drivers need to make complex judgements and perform physical actions that demand high levels of skill and concentration. It is not surprising that accidents happen when people combine drinking and driving, especially when a young and inexperienced driver is behind the wheel.

### 🛑 Crash statistics

In Australia, the legal blood alcohol level for drivers was reduced in the early 1990s. The percentage of alcohol-related fatal crashes dropped from 44 per cent of all fatal crashes in 1980 to 28 per cent in 1997.

## Putting on the pressure

In many countries, campaigners work tirelessly to raise public awareness about the dangers of drinking and driving. They also put pressure on governments to pass tougher laws about alcohol. In particular, they campaign to lower the amount of alcohol drivers are permitted to have in their blood (known as the "blood alcohol concentration" or "BAC"). In the United States, the **pressure group** MADD, which stands for Mothers Against Drunk Driving, have played an important role in persuading US states to reduce legal limits.

▌If people combine drinking and driving, a "fun" night out can end up like this.

## Renée's story

One night, sixteen-year-old Renée Peter was heading for home after seeing a film with friends. The next thing she remembered was lying in an ambulance in such pain that she couldn't even cry. Her family rushed to the hospital to learn that her pelvis had been broken and her face badly cut ... They also learned that Renée had been hit by a drunk driver. The man who hit her was driving a friend's van – he had smashed his own vehicle in an alcohol-related incident just a few weeks earlier.

This account comes from the MADD website (www.madd. org). Most of the victims whose stories are recorded on the site did not survive their accidents.

# Counting the cost

Everyone in society pays for the problems caused by drink. Medical staff are overburdened, industry is badly affected, and the police have the difficult task of keeping order when alcohol-fuelled violence breaks out. All these services cost millions. But it's not just a question of money ... drinking also costs lives.

## Medical costs

Every year, countless patients are treated for the long-term effects of drinking. The medical services also have to cope with emergencies, such as **alcohol poisoning** and injuries caused by alcohol-related violence. But the biggest problem of all is accidents caused by **drink-driving**. Not only do medical teams need to respond to emergencies, but they also have to provide years of care for accident victims.

❚ Medical staff work around the clock to deal with the problems caused by alcohol.

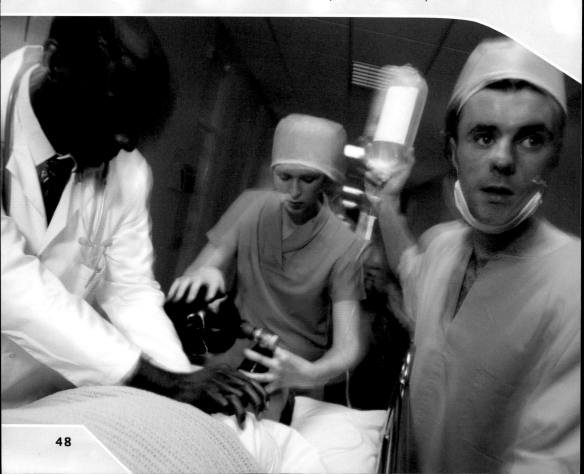

## Costs to industry

Industry also pays a heavy price for the problems caused by alcohol. Millions of working days are lost each year as people stay away from work because of **hangovers** or alcohol-related illnesses. Even if people make it into work, their ability to work well is often seriously affected by the harmful effects of alcohol on their bodies.

## Choices for governments

Some anti-alcohol campaigners say that, given the enormous cost of paying for problems caused by alcohol, it would be better for governments to ban drink altogether. But no Western government has taken this drastic step in recent years. Instead, governments put high taxes on alcohol. This tax goes directly to the government, to be spent on public services, such as the health service and the police.

Governments claim that by adding taxes to alcohol and making it more expensive, they are discouraging people from buying too much. But not everyone agrees with this argument. Some people say that people will buy drink anyway, and that, by making it so expensive, the government is forcing heavy drinkers to spend money on alcohol that should be going on food for their families.

# Viewpoints

Some campaigners believe that our society would be better off without alcohol, but many other people do not agree.

- **Society pays too high a price for alcohol**
  Alcohol costs our society so much money and creates so many problems that it just isn't worth it. It might take a while to adjust to a world without alcohol, but in the end we would all be much happier without it.

- **Alcohol is part of our society, and we just need to handle it carefully**
  We have been living with alcohol for thousands of years, and for most people it's just part of life. We need to concentrate on finding better ways to control its use and deal with the problems it causes.

**What do you think?**

# Help and advice

Are there things that worry you about alcohol? If there are –
either now or in the future – there are lots of people and
places to contact. Many organizations offer help and advice
on alcohol and drink-related problems. You can call a
telephone helpline at any time, and there are trained
counsellors who can talk through problems and help you find
solutions. You can find out more information about people
and places to contact at the back of this book.

## Someone to talk to

Sometimes it can be hard to talk to people you know about the
things that are worrying you. You may want to discuss your
concerns **in confidence**, knowing that whatever you say will not
be passed on to anyone you know. You may also feel that you
need some expert advice.

Fortunately, there's an easy way to find somebody sympathetic
to talk to. You don't have to have an alcohol problem yourself to
call a helpline. If you are worried about someone else's problem
with alcohol, you don't have to keep your concerns to yourself
and try to cope on your own. Helplines are staffed by specially
trained advisers who will be very understanding. They will listen
carefully to your worries and offer you advice and support.

> "One night I came home and found Mum crying. I could see
> she'd been drinking a lot, and it took me ages to get her into
> bed. Then I sat around and wondered what to do. In the end
> I called a helpline. The woman at the other end was great.
> She really helped me get through that night."
>
> Jade, the teenage daughter of an **alcohol-dependent** mother

You will find details of telephone helplines on pages 54–55 of this book. Some helplines are open 24 hours a day, which means you can call them at any time – even if you have a problem in the middle of the night.

## Finding out more

If you just want to find out more about alcohol and the problems associated with it, you can start by contacting the organizations listed at the back of this book. Many of them have useful websites and some supply information packs. Some organizations have local branches, and they will also provide useful advice about people you can contact.

## It's up to you

In the end, it's up to you to make up your own mind about alcohol. You should never feel pressured into drinking if you don't want to. It can also help if you speak your mind and let people know how you feel – you can't control what others do, but you can make your own decisions. After all, you are the only person who knows what feels right and comfortable for you.

▮ Group discussions can be a very good way to share your thoughts and concerns.

# Glossary

**addiction** condition in which a person is unable to manage without a drug and finds it extremely hard to stop using it

**alcohol abuse** drinking dangerously large quantities of alcohol

**alcohol dependence** state of being unable to manage without alcohol

**alcohol poisoning** state that drinkers reach when they have had so much alcohol that their body ceases to function and they become unconscious

**alcoholic** someone who cannot manage without alcohol

**alcopop** sweet alcoholic drink, usually made up of a mixture of spirits and fruit juice

**binge drinking** drinking large quantities of alcohol in a short space of time

**blood pressure** pressure of the blood as it circulates around the body

**breathalyser** device for testing how much alcohol there is in someone's body

**calorie** unit for measuring the amount of energy in food or drink

**circulation** movement of blood around the body

**cirrhosis** disease in which the living tissue in the liver dies and is not replaced

**coma** state of deep unconsciousness from which it is very hard or impossible to wake a person

**concentrated** very strong

**dehydration** the loss of water from the body

**depressant** substance that slows down the activity of the brain and the body

**dilute** make weaker

**diuretic** substance that causes a person to urinate frequently

**drink-driving** driving a vehicle while under the influence of alcohol

**ethanol** pure alcohol

**fertility** ability to create babies

**foetus** baby that is developing inside its mother's womb

**hallucination** experience of seeing or hearing something that is not really present and only exists in the mind

**hangover** combination of unpleasant symptoms that people experience after they have drunk too much alcohol

**happy hour** period (an hour or longer) in a pub or bar during which cut-price drinks are served

**in confidence** privately, without telling anyone else

**inflammation** when part of the body becomes swollen, reddened, and painful

**inhibition** feeling or fear that holds someone back from expressing their feelings or stops them from behaving naturally

**media** TV, cinema, magazines, and newspapers, and any other forms of mass communication

**moderation** avoidance of excess or extremes; drinking in moderation is drinking within reasonable limits

**opening hours** hours when a pub or bar is open for serving customers

**panic attack** sudden very strong feeling of anxiety, which makes a person's heart race

**pressure group** group of people who work together to try to get things changed by constantly putting their views to people in power

**psychological** connected with the mind, for example feelings and moods

**redundant** dismissed from work because you are no longer needed

**rehabilitation** process of returning to ordinary, healthy life after a period of addiction

**sedative** drug which causes someone to become calm or sleepy

**sober** not under the influence of alcohol

**sperm** male reproductive cells

**spiking** practice of adding alcohol or other drugs to a person's drink without their knowledge

**spirits** strong alcoholic drinks, such as gin, whisky, and vodka

**sponsorship** giving money to a person or organization to fund a project, activity, or event, sometimes in return for advertising

**STI** (sexually transmitted infection) infection that is spread through sexual activity

**suppress** to control something firmly or stop it from happening

**toxin** poison

**ulcer** open sore that heals very slowly

**under age** below the legal, or allowed, age for doing something

**withdrawal** process of ceasing to take a substance to which one is addicted, often with unpleasant physical and mental effects

# Contacts and further information

There are a number of organizations that provide information and advice about alcohol. Some have helpful websites, or provide information packs and leaflets, while others offer help and support over the phone.

## Contacts in the UK

**Adfam**
Waterbridge House, 32–36 Loman Street, London SE1 0EH
Tel: 020 7928 8898
**www.adfam.org.uk**
Adfam is a national charity that gives confidential support and information to families and friends of drug users. They also run family-support groups.

**Al-Anon Family Groups**
61 Great Dover Street, London SE1 4YF
Tel: 020 7403 0888 (Helpline)
**www.al-anonuk.org.uk**
This division of Alcoholics Anonymous offers support to the families of alcohol dependents. It puts people in contact with local support groups and makes special referrals to Alateen groups, which offer support to the children of alcoholics.

**Alcohol Concern**
Waterbridge House, 32–36 Loman Street, London SE1 OEE
Tel: 020 7928 7377
**www.alcoholconcern.org.uk**
Alcohol Concern provides information and encourages debate on the wide range of public policy issues affected by alcohol.

**Alcoholics Anonymous (AA)**
PO Box 1, Stonebow House, Stonebow, York YO1 2NJ
Tel: 01904 644026
Helplines: Local AA helplines are listed in all telephone directories.
**www.alcoholics-anonymous.org.uk**

Alcoholics Anonymous is run mainly by people with a history of drink problems themselves, who draw on their own experiences to offer help and advice.

**Campaign Against Drinking and Driving (CADD)**
14 Fontmell Court, Stockwood, Bristol BS14 8BA
Tel: 01275 892225
**www.cadd.org.uk**
CADD supports the victims and families of people who have been injured or killed by drunk and irresponsible drivers. It also campaigns for safer laws on drinking and driving.

**Drinkline: National Alcohol Helpline**
Tel: 0800 917 8282 (9 a.m.–11 p.m. Mon–Fri; 6 p.m.–11 p.m. Sat and Sun)
Gives confidential support and advice on alcohol-related problems.

**FRANK**
Tel: 0800 77 66 00
Email: frank@talktofrank.com
**www.talktofrank.com**
An organization for young people that gives free, confidential advice and information about drugs, including alcohol, 24 hours a day.

**National Association for Children of Alcoholics**
Tel: 0800 358 3456
Offers help and information for young people whose parents have a drink problem.

# Contacts in Australia and New Zealand

**Al-Anon Family Groups**
GPO Box 1002 H Melbourne VIC 3001
Tel: 03 9654 8838
Helpline: 08 8231 2959
**www.al-anon.alateen.org/australia**
See the UK entry for more information on this organization. It also has links to Alateen, a special service for teenagers.

**Alcohol & Other Drugs Council of Australia (ADCA)**
17 Napier Close, Deakin, ACT 2600
Tel: 02 6281 0686
**www.adca.org.au**
ADCA works with the government, business, and community organizations to prevent or reduce the harm caused by alcohol and other drugs.

**Alcoholics Anonymous (AA)**
48 Firth Street, Arncliffe, NSW 2205
Tel: 02 9599 8866
Helpline: 08 8346 3255
**www.aa.org.au**
The Australian division of Alcoholics Anonymous – see information in the UK entry. Many local telephone directories include a number for a local AA branch.

**Australian Drug Foundation**
409 King Street, West Melbourne, VIC 3003
Tel: 03 9278 8100
**www.adf.org.au**
An organization that works to prevent and reduce alcohol and other drug problems in the Australian community. It provides advice to young people about alcohol and drugs, and has a teen website area called Somazone.

**Foundation for Alcohol and Drug Education (FADE)**
9 Anzac Street, PO Box 33–1505, Takapuna, Auckland, New Zealand
Tel: 09 489 1719
**www.fade.org.nz**
A national organization that provides services throughout the country. Has a resource library, fact sheets, books, videos, posters, website, and more for anyone who wants to learn more about alcohol and other drugs.

# Further reading

## Non-fiction
*Alcohol and You*, by Jane Claypool (Franklin Watts, 1997)

*Different Like Me: A Book for Teens who Worry about their Parents' Use of Alcohol/Drugs*, by Evelyn Leite and Pamela Espeland (Johnson Institute, 1989)

*Dr Miriam Stoppard's Drug Information File: From Alcohol and Tobacco to Ecstasy and Heroin*, by Miriam Stoppard (Dorling Kindersley, 1999)

*Drugs: The Truth*, by Aidan Macfarlane and Ann McPherson (Oxford University Press, 2003)

*Let's Talk about Alcohol Abuse*, by Marianne Johnston (Rosen Publishing Group, 1997)

*Need to Know: Alcohol*, by Sean Connolly (Heinemann Library, 2000)

*Why do People Drink Alcohol?*, by Julie Johnson (Hodder Wayland, 2000)

## Fiction
*God of Beer*, by Garret Keizer (HarperCollins Publishers, 2002)

*Tears of a Tiger*, by Sharon M. Draper (Atheneum, 1994)

# Further research

If you want to find out more about problems related to alcohol, you can search the Internet, using a search engine such as Google. Some useful keywords to try are:

Alcohol + health
Alcohol + driving
Alcohol + families
Alcohol + law
Alcohol dependence
Binge drinking

**Disclaimer**
All the Internet addresses (URLs) given in this book were valid at the time of going to press. However, owing to the dynamic nature of the Internet, some addresses may have changed or sites may have ceased to exist since publication. While the author, packager, and publishers regret any inconvenience this may cause readers, no responsibility for any such change can be accepted by the author, packager, or publishers.

# Index